KHAWAJA

Paul Kelly is one of Australia's favourite singer songwriters. He was born in Adelaide, one of nine children, in 1955. He has been making records since 1978, has collaborated with other songwriters and performers, and has composed music for film and theatre. In 2010, he published his bestselling memoir, *How to Make Gravy*.

Paul is a passionate Test cricket fan who has written three songs about cricketing legends – Don Bradman, Shane Warne and, now, Usman Khawaja.

Avinash Weerasekera grew up in Sri Lanka, but now lives in Melbourne. He is an accomplished commercial illustrator, cartoonist and fine artist. He previously drew street portraits and caricatures, and studied Architecture at RMIT University.

He recently published his debut book, *What to Expect When You're Immigrating*, a collection of cartoons and social commentary.

PUFFIN BOOKS

We acknowledge that Aboriginal and Torres Strait Islander peoples are the Traditional Custodians and the first storytellers of the lands on which we live and work. We honour Aboriginal and Torres Strait Islander peoples' continuous connection to Country, waters, skies and communities. We celebrate Aboriginal and Torres Strait Islander stories, traditions and living cultures; and we pay our respects to Elders past and present.

PUFFIN BOOKS

UK | USA | Canada | Ireland | Australia
India | New Zealand | South Africa | China

Penguin Random House Australia is part of the Penguin Random House group of companies whose addresses can be found at global.penguinrandomhouse.com.

First published by Puffin Books, an imprint of Penguin Random House Australia Pty Ltd, in 2023

'Khawaja' written by Paul Kelly, Hank Williams and Fred Rose
Based on 'Kaw-Liga' written by Hank Williams and Fred Rose
© Sony Music Publishing Australia (Australia) Pty Limited / Sony/ATV Milene Music
Licensed by Sony Music Publishing (Australia) Pty Limited

Illustrations copyright © Avinash Weerasekera, 2023

Design by Tony Palmer © Penguin Random House Australia Pty Ltd
Printed in China

Author photography by Michael Hili
Illustrator photography by Temitope Adesina

 A catalogue record for this book is available from the National Library of Australia

ISBN 978 1 76 1340611 (Hardback)

Penguin Random House Australia uses papers that are natural and recyclable products, made from wood grown in sustainable forests. The logging and manufacture processes are expected to conform to the environmental regulations of the country of origin.

penguin.com.au

KHAWAJA

WORDS BY
PAUL KELLY

Illustrations by
Avinash Weerasekera

PUFFIN BOOKS

Khawaja loved the game of cricket, since he was a boy.

With his good friend Davey, it was their pride and joy.

KHAWAJA-A-A-A!

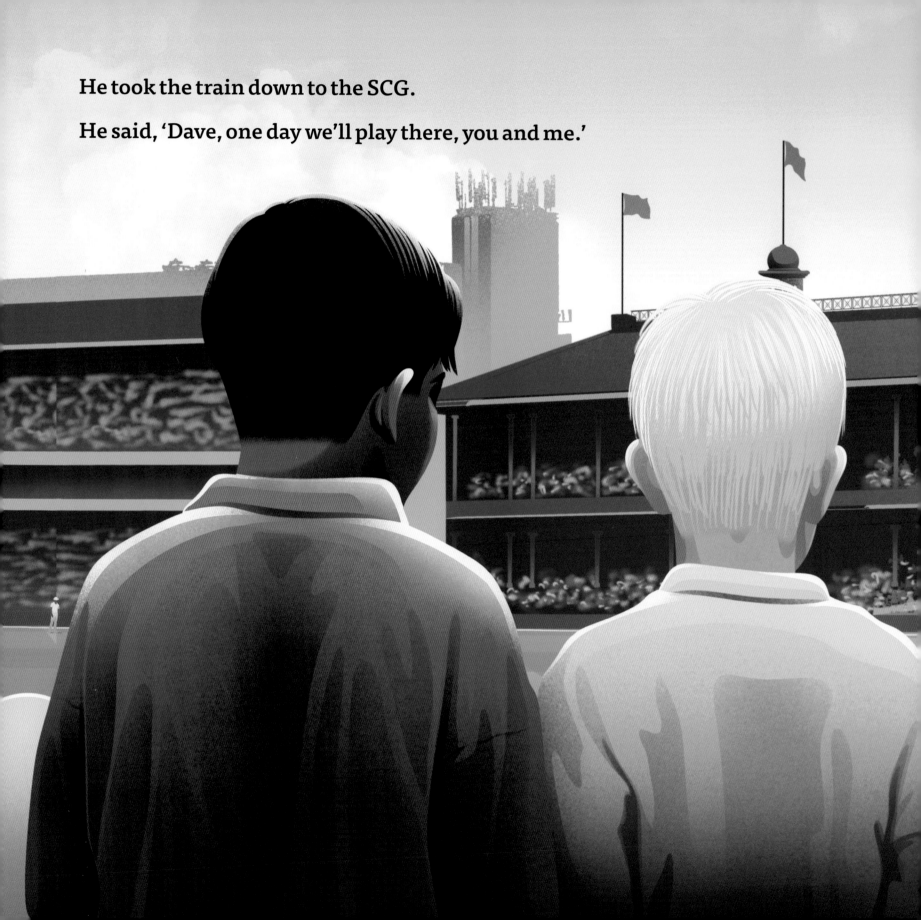

He took the train down to the SCG.

He said, 'Dave, one day we'll play there, you and me.'

He loved his bat and ball and gloves.

He loved his batting pads.

He played a million weekend games
in front of mums and dads.

KHAWAJA-A-A-A!

Cricket lit a fire, deep in his soul.
And every day he worked on his control.

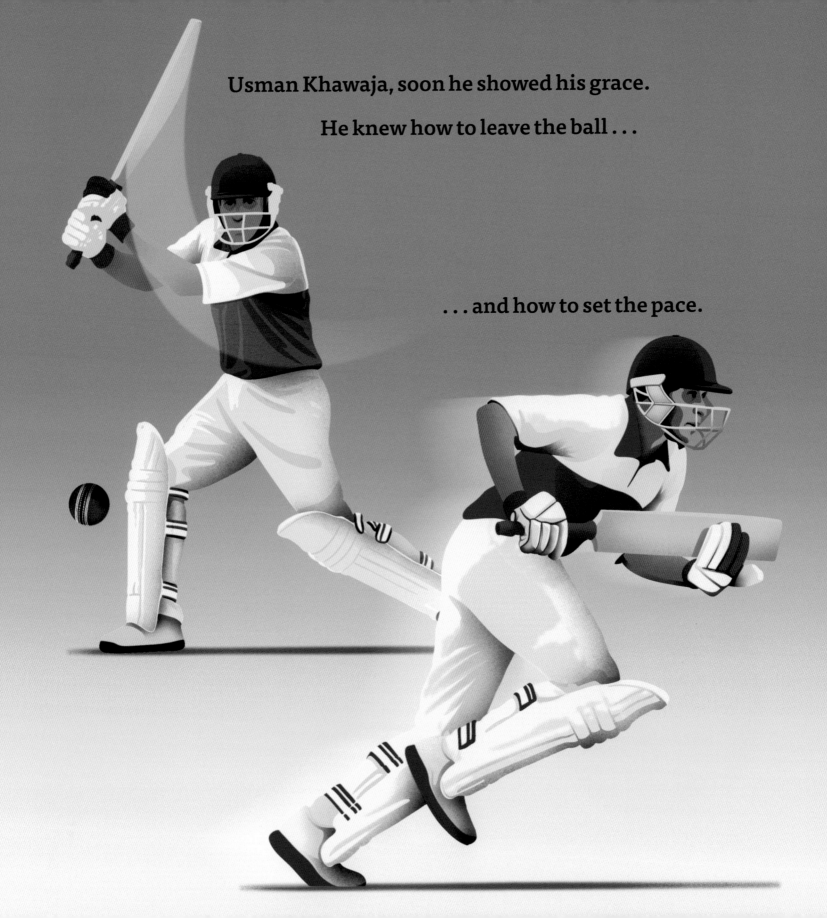

Usman Khawaja, soon he showed his grace.

He knew how to leave the ball . . .

. . . and how to set the pace.

He set himself to conquer...

...and...

SPEED

SWING

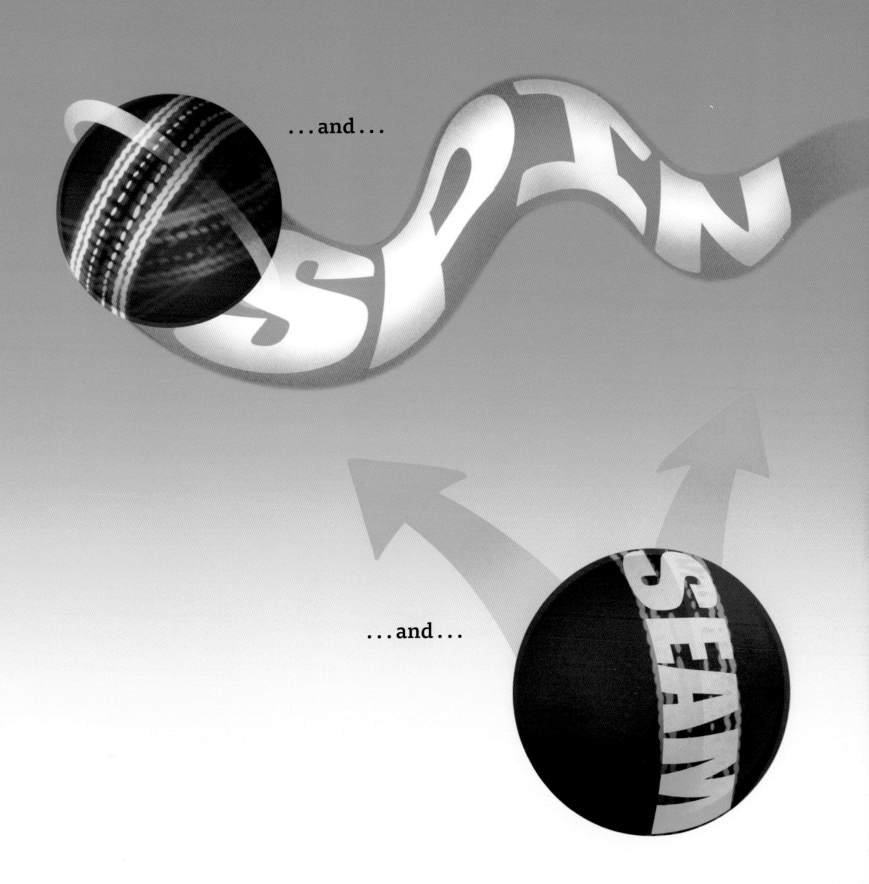

...and...

...and...

Before too long,
he made the national team!

Khawaja pretty soon found out
that when you reach the top,
it's only temporary –

everybody wants your spot.

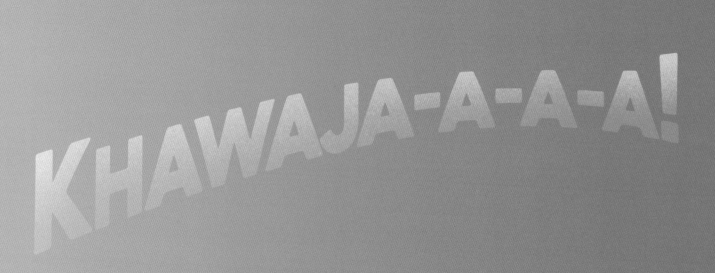

For reasons we don't always know,
selectors say 'yes', sometimes . . .

. . . then say 'no'.

And at the age of 35, when most thought he was through, he got some luck and got the call and to himself stayed true.

KHAWAJA-A-A-A!

At the SCG, he made a stunning ton.

100 100

Then backed it up with an even better one!

Usman Khawaja, a man of grit and grace.
He knows when to take his time and when to up the pace.

Many other batsmen love to land a blow,
but Usman's all about the flow.

Usman Khawaja, the boy's still in your face.

To many you bring joy and make the world a better place.

Triumph and disaster, you treat them equally . . .

Uzzy, you'll go down in history.

ABOUT THE SONG

By 2022, **Usman Khawaja** had already achieved so much. He was the first Muslim and the first Pakistan-born cricketer to play Test cricket for Australia. He had represented NSW and Queensland, played for Australia in Tests, One Day and T20 Internationals, as well as qualified as a pilot. He had even started a charitable foundation and was working to make cricket more inclusive. He was happily married with one gorgeous daughter and another on the way. But he had been dropped from the national side and didn't think he would ever play Test cricket again . . .

So when he returned to the field in 2022, he was determined to show the world what he could do. It seemed like everyone in Australia watched spellbound as Khawaja picked up the bat and made Ashes history, scoring centuries in both innings of the New Year's Test at the SCG. It was exactly what Australia needed after two terrible years of lockdowns and Covid.

Overnight, Usman Khawaja became one of the most recognised faces in Australian sport, a household name and a national hero.

Watching that day was Australian music legend and Test cricket fan, **Paul Kelly**. He was inspired to write a song celebrating Khawaja's extraordinary story. With a tune taken from a Hank Williams song, he took to social media to perform it, and before long it had been shared around the world, viewed tens of thousands of times and made the international news.

You can sing along to Paul's original performance at: youtube.com/watch?v=jlQG4LLgivg

A studio audio version is also available on all streaming services.